When Someone You Love Dies, What's Next?

When Someone You Love Dies, What's Next?

A Practical Guide to Funerals, Finances, Estates and More

Susan Rutledge

WILLOW
BEND
PRESS

When Someone You Love Dies, What's Next?
Copyright ©2021 by Susan Rutledge.
Published by Willow Bend Press, Prosper, TX
www.susanrutledge.com

All rights reserved. No part of this publication may be reproduced, stored in a retrieval system or transmitted, in any form or by any means—electronic, mechanical, photocopying, recording or otherwise, without prior written permission from the publisher, except for the inclusion of brief quotations in a review.

Scripture quotations marked ESV are from the ESV® Bible (The Holy Bible, English Standard Version®), copyright ©2001 by Crossway, a publishing ministry of Good News Publishers. Used by permission. All rights reserved.

Scripture quotations marked NLT are taken from the Holy Bible, New Living Translation, copyright ©1996, 2004, 2015 by Tyndale House Foundation. Used by permission of Tyndale House Publishers, Carol Stream, Illinois 60188. All rights reserved.

Every effort has been made in the creation of this book to provide accurate information. However, this book reflects only the opinion and experience of the author and is offered without warranty. Regulations change, vary from state to state and country to country. Seek professional advice prior to making any legal or financial decisions. Neither Willow Bend Press nor the author shall have any liability to any person or entity in regards to any loss or damage caused or alleged to be caused directly or indirectly by the information in this book.

Paperback ISBN-13: 978-1-950019-18-2
Electronic ISBN-13: 978-1-950019-19-9

First Printing April 2021

Cover Photograph by Aiden Guinnip

Library of Congress Control Number 2021903579

Publisher's Cataloging-in-Publication Data

Names: Rutledge, Susan, author.
Title: : When someone you love dies , what's next? A practical guide to funerals , finances , estates and more / Susan Rutledge.
Description: Prosper, TX: Willow Bend Press, 2021.
Identifiers: LCCN: 2021903579 | ISBN: 978-1-950019-18-2 (pbk.) | 978-1-950019-19-9 (ebook)
Subjects: LCSH Inheritance and succession. | Estate planning. | Wills. | Death. | Funeral rites and ceremonies. | BISAC SELF-HELP / General | FAMILY & RELATIONSHIPS / Death, Grief, Bereavement | LAW / Estates & Trusts
Classification: LCC KF750.Z9 .R88 2021 | DDC 346.7305/2--dc23

This book is dedicated to Rev. Joe Slaughter, a man greatly gifted with compassion and the ability to minister to grieving families. Thank you for mentoring me!

About the Author

Susan Rutledge served in ministry to children and families for more than thirty years. During that time, she walked through the death of a loved one with dozens of families, including her own. ***When Someone You Love Dies, What's Next?*** embodies her desire to share knowledge, experience and direction with those who need it the most.

Susan and her husband Grant reside in Prosper, Texas. They have four married children and 11 grandchildren. Susan retired in 2011 to spend more time with family and pursue a life-long dream of writing.

Other books by Susan Rutledge include ***Simple Words to Love By***, ***Critter Wisdom for Humans***, ***Our Journey to You—A Newborn Adoption Journal***, ***The Cares and Prayers Journal for Tweens***, and four children's books: ***Barely a Bunny***, ***Marvin Maples Told a Lie***, ***Have You Seen the Missing Letter A?*** and ***Ty the Turtle in the Land of the Can'ts***.

For more information, go to susanrutledge.com.

"I pray that God, the source of hope, will fill you completely with joy and peace because you trust in Him. Then you will overflow with confident hope through the power of the Holy Spirit."
Romans 15:13 NLT

Contents

Preface 1

Introduction 3

Funerals, Memorials and Burials 5

    Service & Burial Options 7

    Choosing a Funeral Home 8

    List of Services 9

    The "Funeral Rule". 10

    Methods of Payment 12

    Tips for Lowering Costs 13

    Burial Options 14

    Purchasing a Cemetery Plot 15

    National Cemeteries 15

    Grave Markers 17

    Notifying Family & Friends 18

    Planning the Service 19

    Church Funerals. 20

    Non-Church Options 20

    Service Element Suggestions 21

    Open or Closed Casket? 22

    Viewing Options 23

    Writing the Obituary. 24

    Honorariums 25

    House Sitters. 25

The Death Certificate, Will, Probate and Insurance. 27

    Death Certificate Details. 28

    Ordering Death Certificates. 29

Contents

    Wills & Probate 30
    What You'll Need 31
    Life Insurance Policies 32
    Other Insurance Benefits 33
    Insurance Coverage 33
Notifications and Cancellations 35
    Guard Against Identity Theft 36
    Collect Unpaid Wages 37
    Care Facility Refunds 37
    Stop Recurring Payments 37
    Mail 38
    Canceling Services 38
    Subscriptions & Memberships 39
    Credit Cards 39
    Financial Institutions 40
    Retirement Accounts 40
    Mortgages 41
    Changing a Joint Tenancy Deed 41
    Vehicle Loans 42
    School Loans 42
    Benefit Income 42
    Property Insurance 43
    Email Accounts 43
    Social Media Accounts 43
The House, Pets and Personal Items 45
    The House 46

Contents

Pets 47

Landscape and Plants 47

Pool Equipment 47

Vehicles 47

Medications. 48

Medical Supplies & Equipment 48

Leased Vehicles. 49

Miscellaneous. 49

Tracking Down Assets. 50

Unclaimed Property 50

Hidden Cash. 51

Safety Deposit Boxes 51

Money Transfer Accounts. 53

Cash Back Credit Rewards 53

Help & Acknowledgments 55

Enlist Family & Friends. 57

Gifts of Food. 58

Plants & Flowers. 58

Kindness & Support. 59

Contact Information & Notes 61

Contact Information 62

Credit Reporting Agencies 62

Notes 63

Preface

The death of a loved one, whether sudden or expected, is seldom easy. A tremendous feeling of loss, combined with the pressures of making final arrangements, can be overwhelming. At a time when you feel numb and vulnerable, people will be looking to you for answers and a plan.

When Someone You Love Dies, What's Next? is designed to help you know what to expect, who to talk to and which questions to ask as you navigate through the first days and weeks following a death. Use the note pages at the back of this book for jotting down questions, tracking phone numbers and people to call and listing the things that need to be done. Seek counsel, listen to advice and pray for wisdom. Ask God to give you His peace and direction for the many decisions that have to be made.

This is the time to let your pastor, trusted friends and family members help you. Delegate the things you don't have to do, and save your energy for the things only you *can* do.

The recommendations in this book are not intended to represent legal advice. Laws vary from state to state. Consult a local attorney for all legal questions.

> *"If you need wisdom, ask our generous God and He will give it to you..."*
> James 1:5a NLT

Introduction

If you have recently experienced the loss of a loved one, I pray you are surrounded by loving family and friends and that you have a personal relationship with the Lord Jesus Christ to bring you comfort and strength.

People grieve in a thousand different ways and you will too, in your *own* way. Grief isn't a sign of weakness. It's a natural part of life and a by-product of loving someone. Loss hurts and it takes time to adjust to a new normal. I don't discuss emotional recovery in this book, but I do encourage you to be patient with the process. And with yourself.

We learn and grow through life experiences. As you walk through the loss of your loved one, imagine how this same experience will be for your family when you're the one who has died. Consider what you can do *now* to simplify what they will go through *then*.

My good friend Reverend Mel Pugh encouraged me to mention the importance of *planning ahead* for end-of-life services and burial. Pre-need packages can be purchased which lay out personal preferences, prevent financial hardship and take the decision-making burden off of family members. Most pre-need packages are transferable to another funeral home, so even if you move to another city or state, the benefits can still be used. A pre-need package would take care of most of the issues discussed in the first section of this book, *Funerals, Memorials and Burials*.

Allow me to make one more recommendation. Make sure you have a will. If you die without one, the state will assign an executor and decide who your beneficiaries are and how your estate will be divided between them. It can be difficult, expensive and heartbreaking for your family.

These thoughts I leave with you ... equip your family with the tools and details they'll need to handle your affairs when the time comes. Leave a signed and duly executed will, organize important documents for easy access and finally, provide your family with a plan that outlines your end-of-life wishes.

~Susan Rutledge

Funerals, Memorials & Burials

Celebrating the life of your loved one may include a funeral or memorial service preceded or followed by a burial. This section describes different options and helps you navigate the decision-making process.

The first funeral I ever attended was with my grandparents in their old, wood-framed church in Kaw City, Oklahoma. I was probably eight or nine years old at the time and had never seen a dead person before. We sat on a pew toward the back, but I could still see part of the deceased woman's body laying in an open casket at the center front of the sanctuary. I was filled with curiosity.

At the end of the service, we were dismissed row by row to walk by the casket. It was a serene moment but not at all frightening, even for someone as young as me who knew nothing about death. To this day, I recall the image of my grandmother's friend, a native American Indian from the Kaw Nation, dressed in a traditional colorful costume, lying motionless and peaceful with her hands entwined across her chest. She looked like she was asleep.

I'm sure family and friends were sad, but the underlying sense of normalcy conveyed in her service impacted me for a lifetime. Death isn't something to fear or run from. It is a natural part of life.

Over the years, I have been honored to sit at the bedside of many people when they took their last breath. Whether they were strangers, close friends or family, God equipped me to spread His comfort and peace to both the family and the dying as they slip from a broken earthly body into eternity.

Oh how precious those last moments and touches can be! Don't be afraid to draw close when the end is near.

Service & Burial Options

Full Service Funeral – The body is embalmed to allow public visitation at the funeral home and/or a viewing before and/or after the funeral service. It is typically held at a church or the funeral home's chapel, followed by graveside services at the cemetery. The body is transported in a hearse while the family has the option to ride in limousines. An obituary is posted on the funeral home's website, and death notices are sent to local newspapers. Printed programs, special music and video tributes are common.

Memorial Service – Similar to the Full Service Funeral but the body is not present.

Graveside Service – Family, friends and an officiant gather at the burial site in the cemetery for a brief service prior to interment. This may or may not occur following a funeral service at another location.

Direct Burial – The body is buried shortly after death. No embalming is required, but most cemeteries require a casket and vault or grave liner. Graveside services and/or a memorial service can be held at any location and time of your choice.

Direct Cremation – The body is cremated shortly after death. Embalming is not required or necessary. In Texas, you must obtain a waiver from a County Medical Examiner or Justice of the Peace to be exempt from their "48-hour cremation waiting period". A memorial and/or graveside service (if the cremains are to be buried) can be held at any time. No laws govern how and where the cremains can be stored, but local and state laws *may* govern how they can be transported and where they can be spread.

Did You Know?

From the time a Jewish person dies until they are buried, their remains are never left alone.

Choosing a Funeral Home

One of your first decisions will be which funeral home to use. Even if the death of your loved one occurred in another city, choose and deal with the funeral home that will be *receiving* the body and coordinating the funeral. Otherwise, you may find yourself paying for some services twice.

There are two major factors to consider when choosing a funeral home (not necessarily in this order):

(1) **Reputation.** Talk to people you know who have used funeral home services in the area where you live. Ask who they used and what their experiences were. Check with the Better Business Bureau in the town the funeral home is located in. Look for a satisfactory rating and no unresolved complaints.

(2) **Cost of Services.** The average cost of a funeral is over $8,500 which *excludes* burial costs and miscellaneous expenses such as flowers. Many funerals easily exceed $10,000. The difference between funeral homes providing the *same* services can vary from hundreds to thousands of dollars. By law, they are required to provide you with an itemized price list.

If possible, compare the prices of two to three funeral homes before deciding which one you want to use. Although hospitals prefer to have bodies picked up as soon as possible, they will usually hold the body long enough for you to make some phone calls before making a final decision.

Did You Know?
If your loved one was a veteran, there may be benefits and services he or she is entitled to. Be sure to tell your funeral director!

List of Services

The following is a list of services or products that are available through most funeral homes. Take the time to plan what you want before you sit down with your funeral director, so you make informed decisions.

- Filing necessary paperwork
- Securing necessary permits and copies of the death certificate
- Coordinating with life insurance companies to collect death benefits
- Transporting the body to the funeral home, church, funeral chapel and cemetery, including hearse and driver
- Coordinating arrangements with the cemetery or crematory
- Embalming
- Cosmetic preparation of the body
- Use of the funeral home or chapel for a viewing or visitation
- Providing limousines and drivers for transporting family
- Providing a casket and outer burial container or urn
- Providing printed programs for the funeral or memorial service
- Providing a website page to display photos and receive messages from friends and relatives
- Creating a video tribute for the service
- Use of funeral staff for the service at the funeral chapel or another location
- Receiving, displaying and transporting floral arrangements
- Properly storing the body at the funeral home
- Receiving the body from another location
- Cremation
- Writing and submitting obituary to newspapers
- Recording the source of floral arrangements, sometimes including photos of the flowers and a memory book
- Laminated copy of the newspaper obituary
- Printing personalized thank you notes
- Providing a large framed photograph of the deceased to be displayed at viewings, visitations and services
- Police escort to cemetery

The "Funeral Rule"

Making funeral arrangements can be highly emotional. When you meet with the funeral home representative, take along a trusted friend or family member to help you evaluate all your options and make practical decisions.

The "Funeral Rule", enforced by the Federal Trade Commission, is a list of requirements all funeral homes must abide by. Know your rights and what services to ask for or reject *before* you sign or agree to anything. The "Funeral Rule" is summarized below:

A Written Price List of all services provided must be given to you upon request when you visit a funeral home. This list may include package offers, but must also give an itemized list of individual services and their price.

Phone Information on pricing must be provided by the funeral home if you ask for it. You do not have to give them your name or number. They may offer to mail or email a list to you, but they are not required to do so.

Purchase Only What You Want. Package deals may offer some services at a discount, but unless you want everything in the package, you may be better off purchasing each service separately.

See a Written Casket Price List *before* you look at their caskets. Ask about lower-priced products they may not prominently display with higher priced caskets.

See a Written Outer Burial Container List *before* you look at the containers. Outer containers aren't required by state law, but many cemeteries require them to keep graves from caving in.

A Written Statement showing exactly what you are buying and the cost of each item must be provided (along with an explanation of legal or cemetery requirements) as soon as you make the arrangements.

Purchase a Casket or Urn Elsewhere at a significant savings. The funeral home cannot refuse to use a casket or urn you purchase from a casket store or online. Nor can they charge you a fee to do so or require you to be present at delivery. Don't tell the funeral home you're considering the purchase of a casket from a different provider until you have an itemized copy of their price list.

Use An "Alternative Container" instead of an expensive casket for cremation. Caskets are not required by state law for cremation. Funeral homes that offer cremation must make inexpensive containers available.

Embalming is not a routine requirement in any state and adds several hundred dollars to the cost of the funeral. Texas law requires that bodies held for over 24 hours or in transit must be embalmed, refrigerated or encased in a leak and odor proof container. Also, the funeral home may require embalming if the body is going to be publicly viewed. Daily refrigeration costs may be charged.

A friend in my church was the caregiver for his parents. Bill knew when the time came, he and his siblings would have to pitch in to pay for funeral expenses. Much sooner than anybody expected, Bill's father had a debilitating stroke. Death was imminent. Family members were called in to say their goodbyes, and Bill came to my office seeking advice on how to make the final arrangements.

He shared concerns regarding the financial burden of the funeral. We discussed ways to cut costs, and I gave him the name of a casket store which sold quality caskets at a significantly lower price than the funeral homes did. That afternoon, Bill and his siblings visited the store to obtain information and view the casket inventory. When their father died, they ordered a handsome casket from the casket store and had it delivered to the funeral home, at a savings of nearly $2,000!

Methods of Payment

Cash. If you can afford to write a check, ask the funeral home if they will give you a discount for payment in full.

Payment Plans. Most funeral homes offer a financing plan which begins at the time of service even if you are only waiting for death benefits to be paid. Be sure to understand all the details and charges before agreeing to sign anything.

Assigning Insurance Death Benefits. This method of payment is widely accepted by funeral homes. The beneficiary signs benefits over to the funeral home, and *they* contact the deceased's insurance company to collect. A service fee, typically a percentage of the benefit they are filing for, is charged. Never sign away more in benefits than the amount on your statement from the funeral home, even if they offer to return the overage. Also, don't allow them to wrap in the cost of the cemetery. Those costs should be kept separate.

Credit Card. Most funeral homes accept major credit cards. Check interest rates. Your credit card company rates may be cheaper than any payment plan the funeral home has to offer. Using a credit card keeps the funeral home from taking control of the insurance death benefits!

If the deceased already owns a burial plot, provide the funeral home with all necessary information. Unless prior arrangements were made at the time of purchase, the cemetery will charge a fee for opening and closing the grave and for any other services you request, such as providing chairs and a tent for the interment.

> "And the peace of God, which surpasses all understanding, will guard your hearts and your minds in Christ Jesus."
> Philippians 4:7 ESV

Tips for Lowering Costs

A funeral is a major expense and should be treated as such. Don't feel obligated to purchase unwanted services you can't afford. Here are some ways to save and still provide a funeral or memorial service that adequately celebrates the life of your loved one.

- Instead of visitation with the body present, have a reception for family and friends; consider meeting in a church parlor or in your home
- Have the funeral at a church instead of the funeral home
- Have a memorial service without the body present
- Have the family drive their own vehicles instead of using the funeral home's limousines and drivers
- Purchase a casket from an outside dealer
- Ask for a grave liner rather than a coffin *vault but make sure it satisfies the cemetery's requirements for burial
- Use friends and family for pallbearers
- Print your own programs or ask your church to print them
- Use store-bought thank you notes instead of purchasing printed ones from the funeral home
- Purchase flowers directly from the florist instead of ordering them through the funeral home
- Make your own video tribute (make sure the church or funeral home will allow you to use a family-made video)
- Request an immediate burial which forgoes the cost of embalming and several other services

*A vault is a container the casket is placed inside of to preserve it from the elements. State laws do not require vaults. However, many cemeteries require either a vault or a grave liner to keep the grave from sinking as the casket deteriorates. A burial vault surrounds all sides of the casket and offers maximum protection. A grave liner is made of reinforced concrete and covers only the top and sides of the casket. Like caskets, vaults and grave liners can be purchased from outside dealers at a lower price than through the funeral home. Be sure to compare prices.

Burial Options

In-Ground Burial – the body is buried in the ground in an individual "plot", typically marked with a grave marker or headstone. A casket and in most cases, a vault (waterproof outer container for the casket) are required. Some families purchase a group of plots at the same time so they can eventually be buried alongside one another.

Above Ground Burial in a Mausoleum – the body is placed above ground in a secure enclosure located within an enclosed building. The casket will always remain dry so a vault is not required. Mausoleums hold multiple individuals based upon their overall size. They may be publicly or privately owned.

Above Ground Burial in a Lawn Crypt – the body is placed in a secure above ground enclosure located outside. Lawn crypts usually accommodate either one or two bodies.

Cremation – when the body is cremated, cremains can be kept in an urn, scattered in places with special meaning or be placed in any of the burial locations listed above. Some cemeteries allow the burial of two urns in one plot, lowering expenses for the family . Individual cemetery rules may regulate the type of container required.

Cremains can be scattered in most public places and at sea, but some rules may apply. Before scattering any ashes, understand local, state and national regulations. Ask permission before scattering cremains on private property.

Did You Know?

Cemeteries charge you for opening and closing the grave for the interment and for the use of a tent and chairs if needed for the family. If these services were paid for in advance, you should provide paperwork to the cemetery so you don't have to pay a second time.

Purchasing a Cemetery Plot

The average cost of a cemetery plot is between $2,000 and $5,000, depending on the cemetery, the location of the specific plot and the services the cemetery provides. Two cemeteries in the same community may have vastly different prices. Take time to compare them. Ownership of most plots purchased in the United States is permanent no matter how long they remain unused. Many can even be sold to brokers, given or willed to another individual by the holder. However, some cemeteries reserve the right to "reclaim" an unused plot, so understand a cemetery's rules *before* making a purchase.

- What are the terms of ownership?
- What type of grave marker is allowed?
- Is a vault required?
- Is perpetual care of the gravesite included?
- Can flowers and/or other remembrances be placed on the gravesite?
- What is the cost to open and close the grave for interment?
- What services are provided at interment and what is the cost?

Keep all documents regarding the purchase of a cemetery plot in a safe place with other important papers. If a cemetery plot was previously purchased by the deceased, you may need to provide a deed or proof of ownership.

National Cemeteries

Any active or honorably discharged military veteran is entitled to a free gravesite and burial with a government grave marker in a VA national cemetery based upon space availability. That offer is extended to their spouse and dependent children. There is no charge to open and close the grave or to set the marker, but the family is responsible for other costs such as body preparation, casket, the service itself and transportation. Some veterans may also qualify for a burial allowance. Proper documentation including a DD214 form is required. Visit *www.cem.va.gov* for complete information and application forms.

My mother and stepfather lived in a small town in northeastern Oklahoma, five hours away from family. They were enjoying active, independent lives, despite indications Charles was in the early stages of dementia or Alzheimer's Disease.

One day we received word Charles passed out when he stood up from his bedroom chair. Mother was nearby and tried to catch him as he dropped to the floor, but her small frame was no match for his 6'2" frame. He fell on top of her, breaking her wrist and several ribs. While she was hospitalized, the trauma of the accident and her absence from the home catapulted Charles into full-blown Alzheimer's almost overnight. Once mother could travel, we brought both of them to Texas so she could recover. What started out as a temporary rehab visit ended up being a permanent move. For the next several years, we cared for both of them.

Eventually, Charles passed away from the debilitating disease that ate away at his mind and body. He was to be buried in their home town and hospice would help make the arrangements, but first, we had to give them the name of the funeral home to pick up the body.

Fortunately, I knew to have our hospice representative contact the funeral home in Oklahoma where the service and burial would be. That funeral home worked out arrangements with a Texas mortuary who picked up Charles' body, handled the embalming, procured the necessary paperwork and transported his body across state lines. By directly dealing with only the Oklahoma funeral home, we avoided the expense of paying additional charges to a local full-service funeral home in Texas.

Grave Markers

Headstones are placed on top of a grave to identify the individual who is buried in that specific plot. They come in many shapes and sizes, some dating back as far as 3,000 B.C. Headstones contain long-lasting historical information and are often used by genealogists when they research past generations.

A typical headstone contains the full name of the person along with the dates of their birth and death separated by a dash. The headstone of a married or widowed woman may include both her maiden and married name.

Depending on the size and restrictions of the cemetery they are placed in, gravestones may have more than a name and dates. Some are engraved with nicknames, descriptive or loving sentiments, other important dates, religious symbols, an etched photo of the deceased, decorative designs and an epitaph.

Headstones and markers can be purchased from the cemetery or from outside sources. By law, cemeteries are required to accept any headstone that meets its requirements. They must install the headstone if they install their headstones, and they cannot charge you more than if you bought it from them. Before ordering, be sure to find out all requirements including:

- What style/type of gravestone or marker is allowed?
- What are the size restrictions?
- What are the material restrictions?
- What are the color restrictions?
- Are attached flower vases allowed or restricted in any way?

Don't expect to erect the headstone immediately after burial. It will take time to order and have it engraved. And even then, the soil around the grave may need 6-12 months to settle. Cemetery officials can tell you when it's advisable to place the headstone.

Notifying Family & Friends

Make it a high priority to notify family and friends about the death of your loved one as soon as possible, especially out-of-towners who need to make travel arrangements. It is helpful to first coordinate the date of the funeral or memorial service with close family members, your pastor and the funeral home so you don't have to make calls twice. If that can't be accomplished in the first few hours, go ahead and let people know services are pending.

Answering the same questions over and over can be emotionally draining. Ask a family member or close friend to make calls for you. Here are some suggestions of resources you can utilize so you don't forget anybody:

- Christmas card lists
- Address books
- Email addresses
- Neighbors
- Work acquaintances, even if retired
- Organization acquaintances from church, volunteer organizations, clubs, sports organizations, etc.
- Social Media contacts
- Service providers, i.e., hair dressers, barbers, house keepers, in-home caregivers, Meals on Wheels, etc.
- Teachers or students if applicable
- Alumni groups

Consult your loved one's lists as well as your own and encourage the people you contact to spread the word in *their* circle of contacts.

> "All praise to God, the Father of our Lord Jesus Christ. God is our merciful Father and the source of all comfort. He comforts us in all our troubles so that we can comfort others. When they are troubled, we will be able to give them the same comfort God has given us."
> 2 Corinthians 1:3-4 NLT

Planning the Service

Your church's pastoral staff has experience in planning funerals. Contact them immediately. They can provide you with guidance and information.

Where will the service be held? Options include the church, the funeral home's chapel, graveside, public meeting room, etc.

When will the service be held? Depending on the location you have chosen, what are the date and time availabilities?

Who will officiate? If the officiant is important to you, talk to them first before you schedule the date and time of service.

What kind of service do you want? The next few pages describe some of your many choices.

What musicians and music will be sung or played at the service? Did your loved one make any special requests?

How many friends and family are expected? People don't RSVP for a funeral, but you'll need a ballpark figure of how many people you expect in order to select a place with adequate seating.

What notifications are needed? Obituaries typically aren't free and most newspapers only accept them from funeral homes. Either provide your funeral director with the pertinent information or write the obituary yourself, and have the funeral home submit it to the newspaper. Consider submitting obituaries to any city the deceased has lived in.

Are hotel reservations needed? Upon request, some hotels offer bereavement discounts to out-of-town family members attending a funeral. Estimate how many rooms will be needed, make arrangements and forward the information to family members so they know where to make reservations.

Church Funerals

Churches may provide funeral services for church members at little or no cost. Ask which of the following are provided and what the cost will be:

- Pastoral Services
- Receiving flower arrangements prior to the funeral
- Use of the chapel or sanctuary for the funeral service
- Printed programs
- Musicians
- Sound System including video projection and screen
- Audio/Video technician
- Family meeting room
- Meal for the family prior to or after the funeral
- Visitation of the body (the day before the funeral, prior to the funeral and/or immediately following the funeral)
- Maintenance
- Utilities

Make arrangements with your church and pastor prior to setting a date and time for the service. Sit down with your pastor or a church representative to discuss in detail what your plans are and what your needs will be. Make sure you understand and follow any guidelines and restrictions the church has in place regarding funerals and memorial services.

Non-Church Options

Funeral homes usually have a chapel and can arrange for many of the options listed above if a church setting isn't desired or available. Other locations to consider, based on expected attendance, are auditoriums, gymnasiums, office building meeting rooms, gardens, parks and homes. Some families choose to simply gather at the graveside for a few words and a simple prayer. Make the decision that is best for you and your family.

Service Element Suggestions

Funerals and memorial services are for the purpose of honoring the dead and comforting the living. Below is a list of elements you may want to incorporate in the service. This is not an exhaustive list and choices are personal. Take into consideration any requests your loved one may have communicated regarding their service as well as the wishes of close family members.

- Live streaming the service online for those who can't attend
- Meal for family and out-of-town guests
- Reserved seating for family members
- Display photos of your loved one and memorabilia
- Guest book to record attendees
- Welcome
- Open Prayer
- Eulogy
- Favorite music of the loved one
- Favorite musicians
- Congregational hymns
- Sermon
- Video presentation containing photos of the loved one
- Testimonies from family members and friends
- Favorite scripture of the loved one
- Anecdotes about the loved one
- Closing Prayer
- Instructions regarding interment, reception, etc.
- Viewing of the body before or at the end of the funeral
- Reception following the service

Testimonies and scripture readings by family and friends can make the service more personal and meaningful. Set a suggested time limit of three minutes for personal testimonies but know in advance they will inevitably go longer. Ask each speaker to provide you or the pastor with their testimony in writing. It forces them to organize their thoughts at a less emotional time and may help them stay closer to their prescribed time limit.

Open or Closed Casket?

The decision of whether or not to open the casket for either a private or public viewing is a personal one, based upon the family's desires and any previously expressed wishes of the deceased. Below are some of the pros and cons to consider.

Pros of an open casket:
- Provides a level of closure for family and friends
- Allows for family and friends to see the deceased one last time and say their goodbyes
- Family and friends may be comforted in seeing their loved one at peace and no longer suffering

Cons of an open casket:
- May be viewed as an invasion of privacy
- The body of the deceased may be drastically changed from illness or accident
- It is more expensive
- Some religions prohibit it

Pros of a closed casket:
- The deceased is remembered how they were, rather than how their body is prepared by the funeral home
- The date of the funeral must be postponed for any number of reasons; despite embalming, the body may begin to decompose
- The deceased requested it

Cons of a closed casket:
- Some family and friends may have a deep desire to see the body of the deceased one last time
- The deceased requested an open casket

"Blessed are those who mourn, for they shall be comforted."
Matthew 5:4 ESV

Viewing Options

You can specify when and where the casket will be open and when it will be closed. Here are some viewing options:

Private Visitation
A private invitation is extended to individual family members and friends to view the body at a specific time and location, usually at the funeral home prior to the day of the funeral.

Public Visitation
Public notice invites all family and friends to attend a viewing at a specific time and location. Often, the deceased's family members may be present to receive the guests during that time frame.

Public Viewing
The public is notified they can view the body at the funeral home during regular visiting hours, prior to the day of the funeral.

Private Viewing at the Funeral
Individual family members and friends are invited to privately view the body immediately prior to or following the funeral.

Public Viewing at the Funeral
- The casket may be open prior to the funeral for attendees to view the body prior to the service and then closed for the funeral.
- Most churches discourage or don't allow the casket to be open during the service out of respect for the family.
- The casket may be opened immediately following the funeral and attendees are dismissed to file by it if they want to.

Did You Know?

Caskets can be rented from the funeral home for viewing and visitation purposes; when services are over, the body can be transferred into a less expensive container prior to cremation.

Writing the Obituary

Obituaries tell the story of a person's important life events and accomplishments, and provide a genealogical reference for years to come. Begin with the person's name, age, birthplace and date of death. Provide the date, time and location of the funeral or memorial service.

In chronological order, add date and place of marriage including maiden name of spouse, places lived, education, honors and awards, work, military service, hobbies and activities. Details of a previous marriage ending in death are often included. Details of a previous marriage ending in divorce are less common.

If space permits, short anecdotes can be incorporated throughout the person's life details, or immediately following them. These can be humorous or serious memories that provide a window into the life of the person being remembered.

The "Survived By" list should include living family members with their city of residence, how they were related and if applicable, their spouse name in the following order:

- Spouse
- Children in birth order
- Parents *(omit mother's maiden name - see page 36)*
- Siblings
- Grandchildren in birth order
- Grandparents
- Aunts, Uncles, Nieces, Nephews
- Sometimes pets are listed

The "Preceded In Death By" list includes any of the above family members who have already died. Tell how they were related.

The last paragraph may express gratitude for people involved in the care of your loved one. It can also request donations be made to a specific organization "in lieu of flowers".

Honorariums

A thank you note and honorarium, typically in the form of a check or cash, is appropriate for the officiating pastor, musicians and soloists. Your assigned funeral director can give you information regarding the appropriate amounts for your area. If you want to ensure the honorariums are accepted, pay them through the funeral home and have your funeral director distribute the checks to the individuals at the service. If you ask an out-of-town pastor or musician to participate in the service, offer to pay for their transportation, housing and meal expenses, above and beyond the honorarium you give them.

House Sitters

As a precaution, if the obituary of your loved one is published in a newspaper or online, ask a friend or neighbor to sit at the house while the family is attending the funeral or memorial service. Criminals have been known to take advantage of people during life's most difficult circumstances.

> *The night before I was to officiate at the funeral of a dear friend, the family invited me to share a meal with them. Many had arrived from out of town and it was my first time to meet them. When the meal concluded, I gathered his family in the living room, said a prayer and asked each of them to share their favorite memory about the man they knew as husband, father, son, brother and uncle. A special tenderness filled the room for the next two hours as one story led to another and yet another. One minute we were laughing, and the next we were crying, and then we found ourselves laughing again. It was the most perfect way I've ever witnessed a family love and support one another in the midst of a sudden and tragic loss. A sweet man was honored that evening, and I had precious material to share the following morning with a standing-room-only crowd at his service. The greatest lesson I learned that night was how remembering "out loud" can bring comfort and healing.*

The Death Certificate, Will, Probate and Insurance

Information and specific documents will be needed to file for a death certificate, submit a will for probate and file for insurance benefits. Requirements vary from state to state and company to company. This section provides you with lists of what you may need and how to step through these processes.

Death Certificate Details

The funeral home will submit the information needed to register the death and obtain a death certificate. Based upon the state where the death occurred, the following information about the deceased may be needed to complete the form:

- Legal name—first, middle, last, maiden (if applicable) and AKAs
- Gender
- Ethnicity
- Social Security number
- Age at last birthday
- Date of birth
- Highest level of education attained
- Occupation and kind of business or industry
- Birthplace – city and state (or foreign country)
- Residence – state, county, city or town and zip code
- Complete residence address (identify if it's inside city limits or not)
- Dates and details regarding any military or veteran status
- Marital status at time of death
- Surviving spouse name (if wife, list maiden name)
- Father's name (first, middle and last)
- Father's place of birth
- Mother's name (first, middle and maiden last)
- Name, relationship and address of person confirming information
- Place of death (name, address, city, county, state)
- Method of disposition (burial, cremation, removal from state, donation, entombment, other)
- Place of disposition (name of cemetery or other place and address)
- Name and complete address of funeral facility

Carefully review the form before it is submitted. Make sure names are spelled correctly and that dates and locations are accurate. Making corrections later will cost additional money and be time consuming.

Ordering Death Certificates

The funeral director will order death certificates for you. As a general rule, you will need to submit a valid death certificate (not a copy) to:

- Life Insurance companies – one certificate per policy
- Probate court – you may need more than one if the deceased owned property in multiple states
- Financial Institutions – to close accounts and/or open an account for the estate (plan for one per institution)
- Sale of Property
- IRS, DMV, Social Security Administration and credit-reporting agencies

The average number of death certificates needed is based on the number of assets in the estate. It is always less expensive to order a few extras instead of running short. Certificates usually arrive in 2-3 weeks unless there is an investigation, a required autopsy, or extenuating circumstances such as the 2020 pandemic. Keep them in a safe place.

Additional death certificates can be obtained from your state as long as you meet the state's requirements. Typically you must be an immediate family member, executor or funeral director listed on record. Proper documentation must be provided. In some states a notary is required. You need to know specifics on the death certificate you are requesting. The cost varies from state to state, ranging from $10-$25.

> *A family I know put off meeting with the attorney over the probate of a loved one's estate for two months because they were waiting on delivery of the death certificate. Not knowing how long death certificates took to process, they didn't take any action until a follow-up call from the attorney's office prompted them to call the funeral home. As it turned out, the certificates had been mailed promptly and were lost in the mail. New ones were ordered and arrived within days. Don't hesitate to ask questions when you are in unfamiliar territory. If something doesn't seem right, it may not be!*

Wills & Probate

Depending on where you live, probating a will can take anywhere from a few weeks to several months. Hopefully your loved one left you access to a signed and executed copy. Contact the named executor of the will and provide them with documents needed to file an application for probate.

If you are the named executor, meet with a trusted probate attorney at your earliest convenience. Many probate courts won't allow an executor to appear without an attorney. If you don't have an attorney, ask for recommendations from family and friends or your pastor. Typically, there is no charge for an informational meeting to determine what services are needed. In some cases, probate may not even be the best option, especially if the cost of probating the will exceeds the value of the estate.

The more documentation you bring to the meeting, the better equipped the attorney will be to advise you what your next steps should be. The next page provides a list of documents you should gather and take to the meeting. If the deceased owned and operated a business, ask the attorney what additional information to bring. It is a good idea to take a close friend or family member with you to listen, take notes and help you remember details.

It is customary for an attorney to require half of their fees before they begin the filing process, with the remaining balance to be paid prior to or at the probate hearing.

If your loved one died without a will, the probate court will appoint someone to go through the deceased's personal holdings and property, then the court will determine who the beneficiaries are and how the property will be allocated. Until the process is completed, the assets are generally frozen. In cases of joint ownership with right of survivorship, community property with right of survivorship, irrevocable trusts, etc., some property may not have to go through this process. Consult an attorney to guide you and represent your interests.

What You'll Need

Documents
- Executor's Picture ID and contact information
- Original Will – Must be Signed
- Certified Death Certificate
- All Marriage License(s), if applicable
- All Divorce Decrees, if applicable
- Social Security Number of the Deceased
- Veteran Documentation if deceased served in the military

Financial Summary List and Associated Balance
- Known Debts – Are any of them insured?
- Bank Accounts – personal, joint and business
- IRAs
- Pensions and Retirement Accounts
- Investment Accounts
- Stocks and Bonds
- Trusts
- Life Insurance Policies – Amount and Named Beneficiaries
- Non-cash Investments, i.e., minerals, bitcoins, etc.

Property List
List of individually and jointly owned items and their value, including:
- Homes
- Boats
- Vehicles
- Jewelry
- Antiques
- Royalties
- Rental Property
- Business Property

List of Names
The attorney will need the names of the deceased's spouse, ex-spouse (if any), children and any other beneficiaries listed in will. Include their full names, Social Security Numbers, addresses and phone numbers.

Life Insurance Policies

Gather life insurance policies and promptly contact the companies to stop bank drafts or credit charges for new premiums. If you are the policy's beneficiary, the funeral home will accept assignment of policy benefits to pay funeral expenses.

The insurance company is the final authority on the names of current policy beneficiaries. Even though one person is listed on the policy's original copy, the holder could have changed that name with the company at any time. Note that the beneficiary cannot be changed through instructions in the deceased's will. Life insurance companies are accustomed to confirming beneficiaries with funeral homes so your funeral director may be able to get beneficiary information faster than you can. If the named beneficiary is deceased, the benefits go to secondary or contingent beneficiaries. If none are named, the proceeds are passed on to the deceased's estate.

I served as the executor of my stepfather's estate. During the last years of his life he suffered from Alzheimer's Disease, and I had no way of knowing about life insurances policies he'd purchased decades earlier until I began pouring through old boxes filled with his papers. I discovered dozens of policies but none of the issuing companies were still in business. It appeared they could be worthless, but I was hesitant to just throw them away. I turned to the internet and followed a rabbit trail that led me from one merger, transfer or company name change to another. In the end, I learned all the stacks of policies originated from five initial policies. The policy numbers had changed when the companies did but the value of the policies had not! I found all the information I needed to claim the death benefits. The beneficiary listed on the policies was Charles' deceased first wife, so after her death certificate was submitted, the benefits were added to the cash in his estate and distributed according to his will after probate. A few hours of research netted thousands of dollars which could have easily been lost forever!

Other Insurance Benefits

Your loved one may have small policies that will provide benefits. These could include coverage for:

- Paying off the balance of a credit card
- Paying off the balance of an unsecured loan
- Paying off the loan on a vehicle
- Paying off a mortgage
- Paying a benefit if death occurred accidentally
- Paying a benefit if death occurred from cancer

Other policies may also be in force, provided by employers, banks and credit unions where your loved one was a customer. Hopefully documentation is readily available, but read through contracts and ask questions before paying off debts or closing accounts.

Insurance Coverage

If the deceased owned an automobile or other vehicle that was insured, notify the insurance agent to make any necessary changes in coverage.

If the deceased owned insured residential property that will now be vacant, rules vary state by state regarding the type of insurance required. Again, contact the insurance agent holding the policy to get details so the property is adequately covered.

Did You Know?
After a certain amount of time, based on each state's rules, an unclaimed life insurance policy's proceeds may be turned over to unclaimed funds in the state the holder was last known to live in.

Notifications and Cancellations

Subscriptions, memberships and services should be canceled, debts need to be settled and in some cases, refunds are owed to the estate of your loved one. The list may be long, but this section identifies what to look for and how to get started.

Guard Against Identity Theft

No individual is exempt from identity theft, even after their death. Follow these tips to guard against issues with your loved one's estate.

Credit-reporting agencies – notify all three major credit-reporting agencies. Request a "deceased alert" be placed on your loved one's credit report to guard against new credit being taken out in his or her name. Provide them with any necessary paperwork including a death certificate. Periodically check your loved one's name and Social Security number to make sure there is no new activity.

The IRS – send a copy of the death certificate to the Internal Revenue Service. Use the address the deceased used to mail their tax returns to. This notification flags your loved one's account and indicates they are deceased. When the final tax return is filed, include another copy of the death certificate.

The Department of Motor Vehicles – if your loved one had a driver's license or state issued ID, contact the DMV for your state's specific instructions regarding its cancellation and notification of death.

Social Security Administration – when death information is entered into the state's system, Social Security is notified. Confirm your loved one's Social Security number is marked "deceased" so no fraudulent use of the number occurs in the future. Also, if Social Security benefits were being paid, those must be discontinued.

Obituary – criminals often steal the identity of a deceased person by gathering important details from their obituary. To help prevent this, use a person's age, but never provide their birth date or year in an obituary. Also, leave out their mother's maiden name, which is a common security question needed to obtain credit.

Registrar of Voters – if the deceased was a registered voter, report their death to the voter registrar's office in the county where he or she lived. You may need to provide a copy of the death certificate.

Collect Unpaid Wages

If there was an employer, notify them as soon as possible about your loved one's death. Each company's policies will be different but ask for information regarding benefits that might be available including a company life insurance policy and compensation for accrued time off. If there are paychecks or bonuses due, make arrangements for those to be paid to the estate. Company property, such as keys, an ID badge, laptop, cell phone or vehicle will need to be returned.

Care Facility Refunds

The refund of any payments made to a residential care or assisted living facility after the death of a resident are governed by the original admission contract and state and federal laws. Notify the facility immediately regarding the death of your loved one.

Even if a refund is forthcoming, the proration often begins *after* all personal belongings are removed from the facility. Make every effort to retrieve the deceased's possessions as soon as possible. This may be the time to ask for help from a trusted friend or family member so you don't have to pay for extra days.

The facility may request information regarding who the refund should be issued to and where to send it.

Stop Recurring Payments

In many instances, life and health insurance payments are drafted from a bank account or charged to a credit card on a monthly or quarterly basis. Notify insurance companies to discontinue payments as soon as possible. They generally won't prorate a monthly payment but no future payments should be drafted after proper notification. As an extra precaution, you can issue a "stop payment order" with the bank and/or notify the credit card company.

Mail

If no family member lives at the address of the deceased, a Forwarding Address Change order should be submitted to the post office by the executor. Proof of authorization, typically the court order naming the executor, must be provided. Mail can be forwarded six months, and the forward can be renewed for an additional six months if necessary.

Canceling Services

Determine which ongoing personal and residence-related services need to be maintained and which ones can be canceled:

- Mobile phone
- Home phone
- Cable services
- Internet services
- Wifi plans for electronic notebooks, reading devices and smart watches
- Utilities
- House Cleaning
- Lawn Care
- Pool Care
- Pest Control
- Standing hair and nail appointments
- Maintenance service agreements for HVAC
- House alarm monitoring
- Food delivery
- Bottled water service
- Medical equipment rental
- Mail order prescriptions and/or prescription delivery
- Hunting leases
- Toll tags
- Recurring mail orders
- Software services on electronic notebooks, reading devices and smart watches

Subscriptions & Memberships

Magazine and newspaper subscriptions can be canceled, and sometimes prorated refunds will be issued. The contact information can be found in the publication, usually in fine print on the table of contents page. Be sure to cancel those and any of the following:

- AAA
- Onstar
- AARP
- Amazon shopping
- App and Streaming services (Netflix, Disney, Hulu, CBS)
- Website domains and related website services
- Computer software annual fees (Microsoft, Adobe, etc.)
- Digital training subscriptions (LinkedIn, etc.)
- Cloud Memory Services
- Music subscriptions, i.e. Pandora, Sonos, Apple Music, Sirius
- Audio Book Subscriptions

Paid memberships to gyms, sports and hobby clubs, spas, tanning salons, country clubs and other businesses may offer a refund when notified in writing. The first step is notification. If you wait weeks or months before contacting them, do not expect a refund for any time prior to your notification.

Credit Cards

Every company that has issued a credit card to your loved one should receive notification of death, even if there is no balance due. For a complete list of open credit accounts, request a free credit report from one of the three Credit Reporting Agencies. For credit cards with a zero balance, provide necessary documentation and close the account. Destroy all physical cards. Request a prorated refund if any annual fees were paid. If the estate has to be probated before final bills are paid, communicating circumstances to the credit card company may prevent penalties, additional interest and calls from bill collectors.

Financial Institutions

Provide notification of death to all banks, credit unions and financial institutions your loved one had an account with. It is illegal to write a check, transfer or withdraw money from the bank account of someone (even a spouse) who has died unless it is jointly owned and you are named on the account *or* special arrangements have been made with the bank.

Funds privately owned by the deceased are usually frozen until the executor is authorized by the probate court to make disposition of funds. For accounts that are jointly owned with right of survivorship, funds are not frozen and become the property of the other named person(s) on the account. The financial institution will walk you through the process of removing the deceased's name from the account.

Retirement Accounts

Notify the company managing the retirement account(s) of your loved one that death has occurred. The account should have a beneficiary or beneficiaries named, and as long as they are living, no probate is required. Provide any requested documentation, and the funds will be distributed according to the loved one's instructions.

Named beneficiaries on the retirement account cannot be overruled by a will, regardless of circumstances. If all named beneficiaries are deceased, the retirement account becomes a part of the estate and must go through probate.

"The steadfast love of the Lord never ceases; His mercies never come to an end; they are new every morning; great is your faithfulness."
Lamentations 3:22-23 ESV

Mortgages

It may be necessary to wait until the deceased's estate is probated before arrangements can be made to pay a property mortgage that is individually owed by your loved one. Notify the mortgage company of the death, and find out if the loan has any specific death clauses that you and the executor need to be aware of. Working with the mortgage company until probate is complete won't stop the accrual of interest, but will hopefully prevent penalties and foreclosure proceedings.

If the property is owned solely by the deceased, either the estate will pay off the mortgage, a beneficiary will inherit the house and pay the mortgage, or the house will be sold to pay the mortgage. In some instances the mortgage company may allow a surviving spouse or family member to assume the existing loan.

If you are a joint owner of the property with the right of survivorship the property automatically belongs to you and won't go through probate. If you are unsure about joint ownership rules in your state or how your deed is registered, get professional advice from an attorney. If there is a mortgage on the property and you are a co-signer, you will probably be able to continue paying on the mortgage, but the lender may require you to show proof of ability to pay.

Changing a Joint Tenancy Deed

The deceased's name should be removed from the deed of property held in joint tenancy with right of survivorship. It is a fairly simple process to file an "Affidavit of Survivorship". The surviving owner submits the affidavit and proper documentation to the local county agency that registers property deeds. A legal description of the property, deed details and a death certificate may be needed.

Consult with a local real estate or probate attorney to find out what additional documents are required by your county or state in order to change the deed.

Vehicle Loans

If the deceased had a loan on a vehicle, notify the lender of the death and if payments will be delayed pending probate of the estate. Open communication may prevent penalties or attempts to repossess the vehicle. Find out if the vehicle loan carried any kind of life insurance. If there is enough money in the estate, the executor will pay off the balance of the loan. If not, the beneficiary can arrange to refinance the vehicle loan or the lender will repossess the vehicle for payment.

School Loans

Federal School Loans owed by the deceased will not be passed on to their estate. Once proper documentation is provided to the lender, the debt will be erased. This does not include private school loans which will be treated as any other debt owed by the estate. However, some lenders have been known to forgive part or all of a deceased's private school loans. It will be to the benefit of the estate to make the request.

Benefit Income

A surviving spouse and any dependent children may be entitled to Social Security benefits on behalf of the deceased. Meet with a Social Security representative as soon as possible for information on eligibility and filing regulations. There is a time limit for *applying* for benefits, and you can't collect any *back*-benefits you were entitled to prior to filing. Social Security may also pay a one-time death benefit of $255, but it is not automatic. The beneficiary must file for it within the time limit Social Security has established.

Monthly benefits the deceased received for disability, military service, unemployment, etc. must each be addressed separately. In some instances, a surviving spouse and any dependent children may be entitled to receive those payments. Seek professional advice regarding eligibility and how to make a claim.

Property Insurance

Notify insurance companies that covered your loved one's vehicles and property, or provided an umbrella policy. Adjustments will need to be made and in some cases, refunds will be forthcoming.

Email Accounts

Don't be in a rush to close your loved one's email account(s). He or she may have opted for paperless billing, tax information, royalty receipts, digital subscriptions, etc. that should not be overlooked. Read through emails and monitor the account for a calendar year in the event that some notifications only come annually. You might also want to make a copy of the email addresses.

Eventually the email account should be closed to prevent unauthorized use. If you have the login information, you can close it yourself. If not, contact the provider, and follow their instructions on closing an account. You must provide proof the account holder is deceased along with evidence that you are either next of kin or the executor of the estate.

Social Media Accounts

All social media companies have a strict policy against giving out login and password information, even to immediate family members and executors. If you have login information, you can make changes to an account. However even without login information, when proof of death and verification of authority are provided, your loved one's social media account can either be closed or memorialized. Rules are easily accessed online and vary based on the company. When an account is memorialized, a tasteful notation is placed on the holder's page indicating they are deceased. If the privacy setting on the account allows it, family and friends can post information, comments and memories on the timeline.

The House, Pets and Personal Items

Finding and caring for your loved one's personal items is not an easy task. Important and valuable property is rarely in one place, and you may not even know what all to look for. Be methodical, considerate and respectful as you sort through belongings. And remember ... this part is not a race.

The House

If no one is living in the deceased's home, protect it from burglary attempts and squatters by making it *look* lived in.

- Turn inside lights on and off with programmable timers
- Regularly check the front of the house and remove newspapers, fliers and packages
- Use the existing alarm system or arrange for a monitored portable system that alerts you if someone attempts to break in
- Locate and secure valuables in a safe place
- Keep doors and windows locked including the inside door between the house and the garage
- Use the manual garage door lock or unplug garage door opener
- Don't hide a house key outside

Prepare the inside of the house for temporary vacancy to conserve energy and to prevent bugs, smells and damage.

- Discard perishable food from pantry, cabinets and refrigerator
- Dump the trash
- Wash all dirty dishes including any that may be in the dishwasher
- Run a half cup of vinegar through the garbage disposal
- Ask the executor for permission to donate canned goods and non-perishable food to a local food pantry
- Remove clothes from the washer and dryer
- Keep utilities turned on
- Set the thermostat to 50° in the winter months and 85° in the summer months to conserve energy and money
- Turn down temperature on the water heater
- Flush toilets and turn on faucets 2-3 times per month
- Take precautions during freezing weather to protect pipes
- Prepare the house for seasonal weather changes
- Unplug everything that isn't set on a timer to prevent damage from an electrical storm or power surge
- Remove inside firewood and close the fireplace flue

Pets

If your loved one owned pets, make sure they are fed and cared for until permanent arrangements are made. A pet owner may have already asked a friend or family member to adopt their pet if they die. If not, ask family and friends if they would give the pets a loving home.

Landscape and Plants

If your loved one lived alone, attention must be given to caring for the landscape and plants. Based upon the time of year, mowing, watering and weeding may be required to protect the value of the property. The executor can authorize routine maintenance expenses for the house which include necessary lawn care. Make arrangements to water inside plants or give them to friends or family members.

Pool Equipment

Pools require regular maintenance even if they are not being used. If a pool company has been maintaining the pool, it is a good idea to continue the service until other arrangements can be made. Neglecting the pool maintenance can result in the need for costly repairs.

Vehicles

Most automobile insurance policies end when the policy holder dies, and many insurance companies will not write an insurance policy if the car owner and the policy holder are not the same. Vehicles owned by the deceased are a part of the estate. It's best not to drive them until probate is complete and either the court or executor issue an order to transfer the title to a specific beneficiary. Lock the vehicle and if possible, cover it or park it inside a garage. If it won't be driven for more than 30 days, top off the gasoline tank to prevent moisture from getting in the fuel tank, and change the oil.

Medications

State and federal laws make it illegal to use or share prescription medication. All of the deceased's prescription medication should be properly discarded as soon as possible. The best way to safely dispose of unused pills is to take them to a DEA-designated drop box or a drug take-back site (some take-back sites may not be able to accept controlled drugs). Remove all personal information from the prescription bottle or mark it out with a permanent marker. Search the internet for a location near you or ask a local pharmacist for assistance. Flushing certain drugs down the toilet can cause adverse environmental effects.

Vitamins and over-the-counter medication do not have to be discarded, but check expiration dates before using them. Discard any pills that have expired in the same manner as you do prescription drugs.

Medical Supplies & Equipment

Unless items were purchased, any medical devices and equipment furnished by companies, Hospice or friends must be returned. These may include:

- Home monitoring device for pacemaker or defibrillator
- Electronic blood tester for INR or diabetes
- Oxygen tank
- Hospital bed
- Cane, walker or wheel chair
- Bedside toilet
- Shower chair
- Geriatric recliner
- Nebulizer
- IV Equipment
- Infusion Pumps
- Dialysis Machines
- Suction Machines

Leased Vehicles

If your loved one died during the term of a car lease, the vehicle must be returned, and the estate can be liable for either early termination fees, the cost of all remaining payments and/or an assessment for the difference between the lease amount and the current value of the vehicle. Some contracts may allow the lease to be transferred to a beneficiary, a buyer or a lease swap company. Consult an attorney to determine available options.

Miscellaneous

- Return library books
- Cancel reservations, tickets, cruises and other travel plans made by the deceased and request refunds; file a claim on any purchased trip insurance policies
- Contact the provider of individual or season tickets to exchange them for a prorated refund
- Return unused items to the store they were purchased from to receive a refund, especially if they still have the tags on them or you have a receipt
- Make arrangements to return any rented or leased furniture, appliances, tools, etc.
- Register your loved one's name with the DDNC (Deceased Do Not Contact List) to remove them from commercial mailing lists
- Check the value of all gift cards before discarding them
- Download photos off of digital cameras

> "Let not your hearts be troubled. Believe in God; believe also in me. In my Father's house are many rooms. If it were not so, would I have told you that I go to prepare a place for you? And if I go and prepare a place for you, I will come again and will take you to myself, that where I am you may be also." (words spoken by Jesus)
> John 14:1-3 ESV

Tracking Down Assets

Your loved one may have some assets that require sleuthing to uncover. Carefully examine all papers and documents, leaving no drawer, file cabinet or safety deposit box unopened. Read through bank and credit card statements, investment statements, tax returns, mail and email messages. Look for evidence of income, payments and purchases, titles and deeds.

Unclaimed Property

Billions of dollars in unclaimed cash, benefits and property are held by states and federal agencies because they have been forgotten by the owner, or the owner is deceased and the beneficiaries of his or her estate don't know about them.

Periodically, check the unclaimed property websites in any states your loved one may have lived in or had property in. It can take several years for property to appear.

The search engine treasuryhunt.gov can help you find savings bonds your loved one may own that are over 30 years old and no longer earning interest.

Filing a claim varies from state to state. Promptly supply all documentation requested to prevent your claim from being closed. It can be a hassle to reopen a claim that the state has closed.

> ### Did You Know?
> Thousands of storage units are abandoned by renters each year and their contents are auctioned off. If your loved one rented a storage unit, make certain monthly payments continue until the contents are disbursed.

Hidden Cash

Check the pockets and drawers of all clothing and furniture before you give it away or discard it. Your loved one may have hidden cash and valuables in unconventional places. Hidden cash has been found in attics, freezers, between the pages of books, etc.

Safety Deposit Boxes

Your loved one may have valuables stored in a Safety Deposit Box. The contents are a part of the estate and must be reported with the other assets. If you find a key with a number on it, this may be a clue to look for a safety deposit box nobody knew about.

True Stories...

Years ago, my next door neighbor confided in me that she hid all her valuable jewelry in the hem of her curtains, and if anything happened to her, I should let the family know where to find it. I hope she told someone else after I moved.

A couple I know was cleaning out the personal belongings of their deceased parents. In an old cardboard cigar box, they discovered a bracelet in the midst of junky nicnacks. It looked like costume jewelry and almost went into the donate pile, but at the last minute they decided to take it to a jeweler for an appraisal. And what a good decision that turned out to be. The bracelet was identified as a rare and valuable piece of jewelry!

An elderly man who lived during the Great Depression, banded dozens of rolls of large denomination paper money, wrapped them in brown paper bags and hid them inside full cereal boxes, sacks of flour, containers of sugar and bags of dried beans. It was only by accident the first roll was discovered, prompting family members to open and search every container in the house.

I have a precious friend who recently lost her husband after his long battle with a difficult illness. Before John became ill, he was an avid fly fisherman. When he wasn't standing in waders on the river, he was home tying specialized fishing lures in anticipation of the next time he would be. Over the years he made hundreds of lures and accumulated a lifetime of supplies, few of which were of interest to anyone not devoted to that particular sport.

Instead of throwing the boxes away or donating them to a charity that wouldn't know what to do with them, Dianne contacted a friend of John's at the Red River Fly Tying Club for advice. Members came to her home and sorted through the materials, first setting aside rods and fishing gear for the grandsons. Then kits were put together to give to two veterans' groups, "Project Healing Waters Fly Fishing" and "Casting to Heal". These non-profit organizations help disabled veterans with rehabilitation through fly fishing. Additional supplies went to John's fly tying club and to a state park near their home.

What a beautiful example of how a loved one can continue to bless individuals even after they are gone! Whether your task is to clean out a closet, a room or a house, take comfort and joy in distributing your loved one's possessions in a way that helps meet the needs of others.

Money Transfer Accounts

Many people use Money Transfer Accounts to make and receive payments or purchase items. If your loved one has one or more of these accounts, there may be a balance that needs to be transferred into the estate. A few of the popular ones include Venmo, PayPal, Zelle, Google Pay, Apple Pay and Square Cash.

It is wise to conduct a search of all of your loved one's phone apps because chances are, if they used a Money Transfer Accounts, they accessed it from their smart phone. Some of the Money Transfer Accounts maintain a balance while others place money directly into the recipient's associated bank account. The process of obtaining the balance for the estate will vary from company to company. Provide the information each one requires to clear out the balance.

Once balances have been transferred, all Money Transfer Accounts should be properly closed to help prevent loss from identity theft. Be sure to close these accounts *before* you close any associated bank accounts or credit cards.

Cash Back Credit Rewards

Some credit cards offer cash back credit for purchases. Check the statements of your loved one's credit cards to see if there are any rewards programs with balances that have not been redeemed. The executor can apply this credit to the credit card's outstanding balance or request a check be made out to the card-owner's estate.

> "The Lord is close to the brokenhearted;
> He rescues those whose spirits are crushed."
> Psalm 34:18 NLT

Help & Acknowledgments

One way to keep things from falling through the cracks is to allow family and friends to help with the details. Remember to show your appreciation by properly acknowledging their kindness.

A number of years ago, my husband and I drove a friend's wife and two children from Texas to Kentucky to join Mark who was already there, and attend the funeral of his father. It was a two-day trip on icy roads—one the young mother didn't need to make by herself. They didn't ask for our help. We insisted.

The death of Mark's dad was unexpected, but the family had even more to deal with. His mother suffered from Alzheimer's Disease. With her caretaker husband gone, she couldn't care for herself or understand what had happened. In addition to grieving the loss of his father and planning a funeral, Mark had to face bringing his mother home to live with them. Much had to be done in a short amount of time. Fortunately, an army of church friends was ready to roll up their sleeves and go to work. In Kentucky, clothes, toiletries, treasured family keepsakes and bedroom furniture were packed in a van which we drove back to Texas. Friends in Texas helped unload boxes and rearrange furniture so a new bedroom, set up exactly like the old one, was ready and waiting for Mark's mother when they arrived home.

Mark didn't have a choice. He needed help because circumstances were too big to manage alone. It was a blessing for him and for his friends who were privileged to help meet the family's needs.

Even if you have a choice and can get by on your own, don't cheat yourself and your friends out of blessings that come from sharing one another's burdens.

Enlist Family & Friends

The natural instinct of family and friends is to show how they care by *doing* something or *bringing* something to you. The onslaught of people, food and flowers can be overwhelming, especially when you are already dealing with so much change, important decisions, a sense of incredible loss and likely exhaustion.

People would rather do something helpful for you than create a problem, but they need direction. If it's hard for you to ask people to do something, choose a spokesperson and give them a list of things you need. Allow them to answer the calls and assign jobs, even if it's weeks after the funeral. Here is a list of things you might request:

- Making phone calls
- Washing laundry and bedding
- Housecleaning (if you don't want friends in your house, they could pay a service to come in)
- Yard work
- Picking up dry cleaning
- Shopping for groceries or items needed for funeral
- Making repairs at the house
- Pet care, including shopping for pet food, grooming trips, etc.
- Opening and sorting mail
- Writing thank you notes
- Moving heavy objects
- Returning dishes to people who brought food
- Rides to and from appointments
- Lunch dates when things quiet down
- Sorting and taking clothing items to either a resale store or contribution center
- Accompanying you to meetings with lawyer, probate, etc.
- Help with accounting issues
- Accompanying you to meetings at Social Security office
- Assisting you with sale of unneeded items, including cars, sports and hobby equipment, etc.

Gifts of Food

Food is often brought or delivered to you after the death of a loved one, sometimes in dishes that must be returned. Keep an accurate list of the following:

- Food item
- Dish, pan or container it arrives in
- Full name and address of the person who brought the food
- Does the dish need to be returned?

Mail thank you notes, and return dishes in a timely manner.

Plants & Flowers

Plants and floral arrangements are typically delivered to the church or funeral home and transported by the funeral home to the location of the service. If interment immediately follows the service, the funeral home will transport a limited number of the flower arrangements to the cemetery. These are often left at the gravesite. After interment, the other plants and flowers can be taken home, given to friends and family or donated to the church.

Within a few weeks, mail thank you notes to the people and organizations who sent plants and flowers. Include the full name of your loved one in the note so people who don't know your name know who the note of thanks is regarding.

Some funeral homes give you photographs or descriptions of all flowers received along with the card listing who sent them. If they don't offer this service or you'd prefer not to pay for it, enlist a volunteer to take digital pictures of each floral arrangement. Number the pictures, write a short physical description and document who each one is from. Depending on how many flowers you receive, this can be a big job, but these pictures and accompanying list will allow you to adequately acknowledge each one.

Kindness & Support

It is not necessary to mail a written thank you note to everyone who sent a sympathy card or attended the service. However you should express your gratitude with a hand-written thank you note to anyone who did something extra. This might include:

- People who traveled from out of town
- Pall bearers
- Musicians (even if you paid them)
- Ministers (even if you paid them)
- The church (even if you paid a fee)
- Groups or individuals that provided a meal for the family
- People who helped with preparations
- The funeral director who helped you plan the services
- Special nurses, doctors and caregivers who were involved in the care of your loved one
- Friends who visited and provided support for your loved one prior to his or her death
- Anyone who made a cash donation in memory of your loved one

Thank you notes can be as short as 2-3 sentences. The signature can be from you or "on behalf of the family of" your loved one.

People who helped, brought food and sent flowers do not need separate thank you notes. One note expressing your appreciation for everything they did is adequate.

> "Now may our Lord Jesus Christ Himself, and God our Father, who loved us and gave us eternal comfort and good hope through grace, comfort your hearts and establish them in every good work and word."
> 2 Thessalonians 2:16-17 ESV

Contact Information & Notes

This section is designed to help you stay organized by giving you a place to jot down contact information, questions and lists of things to do in one place. Don't try to remember things. Write them down!

Contact Information

Social Security Administration
www.ssa.gov
800.772.1213

Department of Veteran's Affairs (survivor's benefits)
www.va.gov
800.827.1000

National Cemetery Scheduling Office (to schedule a burial)
www.cem.va.gov/burial_benefits
800.535.1117
Fax - 866.900.6417

DDNC (Deceased Do Not Contact List)
dmachoice.org (select "Register the Deceased")

Credit Reporting Agencies

Equifax
www.equifax.com/personal/help/credit-report-deceased-person
Place Fraud Alert on Profile - 888.766.0008

Experian
www.experian.com
Request Reports - 888.397.3742

TransUnion
www.transunion.com
Place a Security Freeze - 800.680.7289

Contact information was correct at the time of this printing.

Notes

Notes

Notes

Notes

Special Request

If you found the information contained in this book helpful, please consider posting a review on Amazon. Even if it's only a few sentences, it would be a huge help. Just log into Amazon.com, search for this book by title, then scroll down to bottom of the screen until you come to the review section.

Thank you!

Susan Rutledge

www.ingramcontent.com/pod-product-compliance
Lightning Source LLC
Chambersburg PA
CBHW042101120526
44592CB00026B/13